DISINTEGRATION

BENJAMIN EMBRY

re
DISINTEGRATION

The Beginning

Not to alarm
You
But I'm not
Feeling well

I'm going
Home

Shining Teethers

No mask

Yellow rubber
Dish washing
Gloves

She rolls
Her
Squeaky cart behind
Me and
Whispers

"Toothbrushes"

Punk Rock PPE

This dude
Is
Wearing
A
Jean jacket

As a

Face mask

Man On The Moon

What is this
Shit
I can't believe you
Don't have
Alcohol
What is this
Shit

You can put a man
On the
Moon
But you can't keep
Alcohol on
The Shelf

I don't believe it
This is
Ridiculous
You can put a man
On the moon
But.....

One second
I'll go get it miss

We just got our
Truck
And haven't had a
Chance.....

Here you go
Limit is
1

Oh
Thank you
Thank
You
Thank you
Thank
You....

Fucking America

You weren't here
You were at
The lake because
Fucking
America

I'm still waiting
For my
Results
What,
Are you
Positive?

And then you are
Laughing at
Me

I don't know
But I think
It's important
I say

You need to
Quit
Watching the news
You
Reply

I smiled
Laughed it off
Walked away
Fuming

Are You James ?

It's all
Bullshit
I'm not
Wearing
One
The president
Is not
Wearing
One
It's
All fucking
Bullshit

Are you James ?
You aren't
James
He told me about
This cream that
I need
But I can't remember
The name
Where is James ?
He said he would
Be here.....

Where is a girl ?
You can't help
Me
You are a man
You don't know
Anything about
Make up
You can't help
Me
You don't know
Anything
There isn't a girl working ?
I need a girl
To
Help me
You don't know
Anything....

Disintegration

I hear a
Cough and
Flinch

A sneeze
No
Mask
In front of
Me

Terror inside

I want to
Scream
Rage
Cry
Scream
Rage
Cry

Cry
Cry

I
Don't
Want to
Die

Because
You are
Stupid and
Insensitive
And
Ignorant
And
Laugh
And
Cough
And
Sneeze
Because
You are
Stupid
And
Insensitive
And
Ignorant
And you

Don't

Fucking

Care

Because you
Think it's a
Fucking
Hoax
A
Fucking
Joke

I
Don't want
To
Die

I'm scared
I'm trying
To hold
Myself
Together

But I'm
Starting

To

Disintegrate....

Rage

She was
Refused
Her medication
I don't know
Why

Her old man
Came in to
Rage

A ruckus
I went to
De-escalate
If I was
Able

Rage man
Walked past me
Muttering
And
Getting
LOUDER

Yelling
About taking us all
Out to the
Woods
And
Killing
Us

Heavy breathing
FISTS
Clenched
He started
Hitting himself
In the side
Of the
Head
As hard as
I have ever
Seen
I walked behind
Him
Aware of those
Others
Around
Me

He left the
Store still
Raging

I

Breathed heavy
With
Relief

Greed

They bought
16
Boxes of
Cereal

Came back
In
Wanted to
Buy

16
More

Greedy

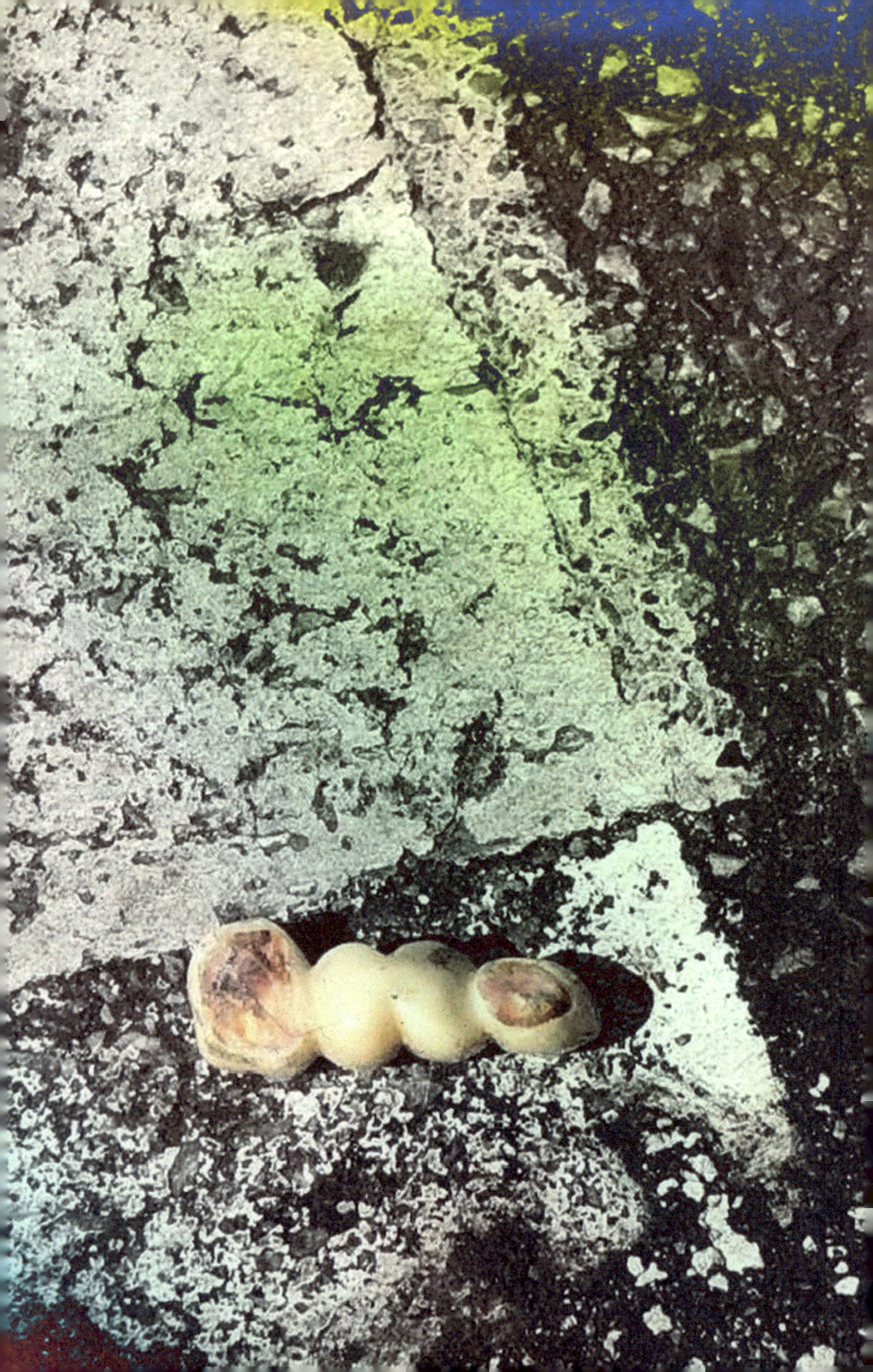

ICK

Outside getting
Carts
A man gets out of his
Truck

He blows his
Nose onto the front
Of his
Already
Stained and dirty
Shirt

Cash Back

No
No
No

I need cash
Back

Sorry sir
At this time
We are
Not
Giving
Cash back
There is an
ATM
For your
Convenience

I don't want to
Use the
Goddamn
ATM
I'm never coming
Back to this
Store ever
Again

The cashier smiled
And checked
Out
The next in
Line

Where Are Your Shoes ?

I look up
To see
A
Child

On the aisle
Of
Candy

Dirty black
BARE
Feet

Is this now
Neglect
And
Abuse

It does not seem
Safe

Lavender Death

A buggy
Full to the
Top

A woman both
Hands gloved

2

Cans of Lysol
Not from our
Shelves

Lavender breeze
Of
Death

As I walk
By to
Lock away
DIRTY
Money

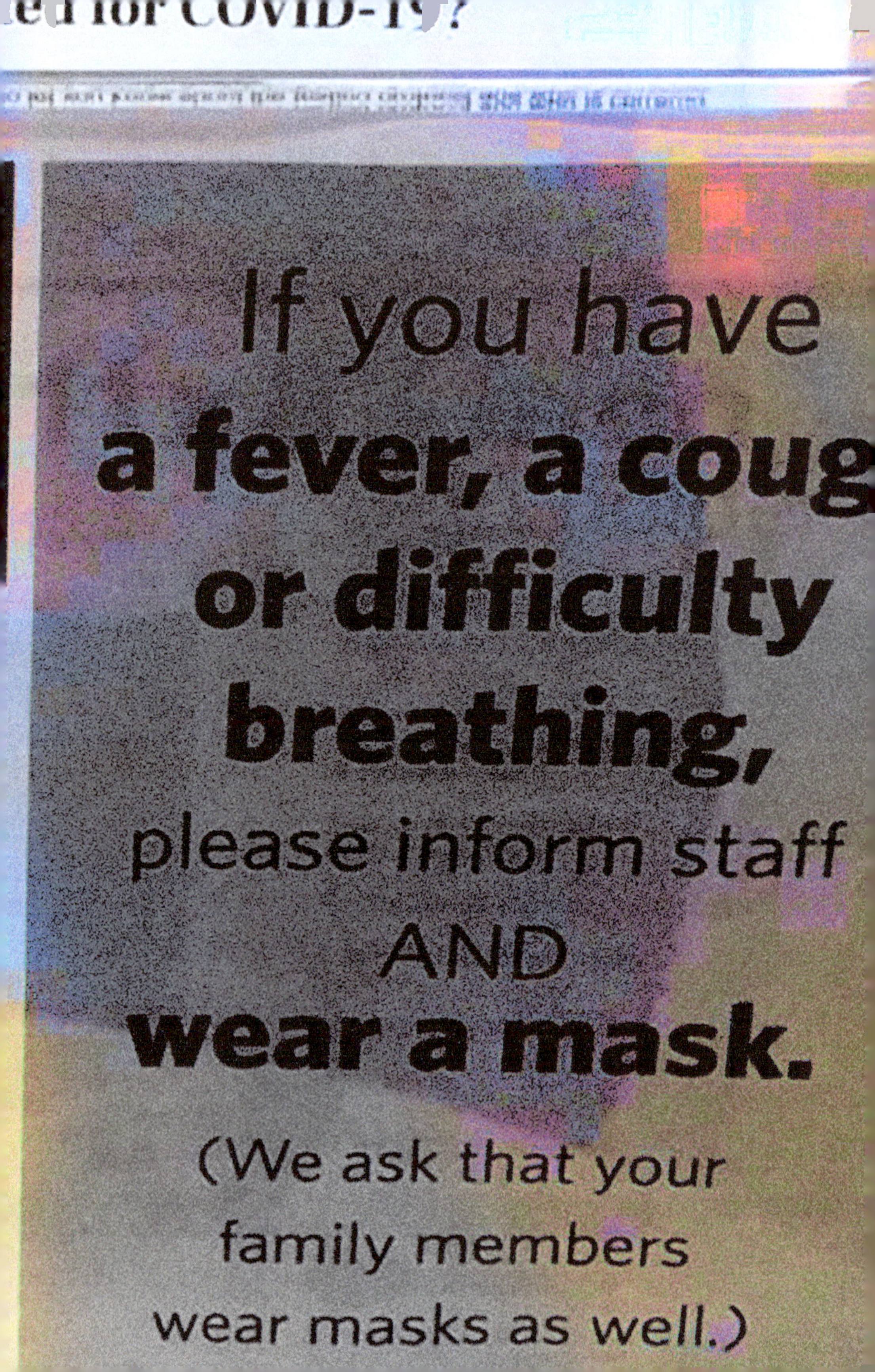

for COVID-19?

If you have
a fever, a coug
or difficulty
breathing,
please inform staff
AND
wear a mask.

(We ask that your
family members
wear masks as well.)

It Is Not Funny

Smashed
My
Elbow

Got to work up front
To
Count money

This lady had
A
Mask on
But
Kept taking it off
Her face

Fucking

Coughing all over
EVERYTHING

Lost my
Mind

Fuckers

I cannot

With these

MOTHERFUCKERS

Right
Now

You Know The Answer, Karen

Hi, thank you for
Calling
How may I
Help you ?

Do You
Happen
To
Have

Any

Hand sanitizer
Face masks
Gloves
Alcohol

No

When will
There be more
In ?

Possibly Thursday
But
Probably not
Because
All of those
Things
Have been
Hoarded

To be sold
Online
At a
Billion %
Mark - Up

You shitty
People

Taking the trash
Out

A truck is
Parked
By the open
Dumpster

An older gentleman
Comes around
The
Corner
With empty
Boxes

That he has
Grabbed
From the top
Of the
Garbage

Hello Sir

We are moving
And I need
Boxes

All of ours
Are
Crushed
I manage to
Find three for him

Not covered in
The filth
Of god knows
What

WASTE PRO
Caring For Our Communities
850-872-1800
www.wasteprousa.com

Happiness Is Not Allowed Right Now

Hey !

Whistling Guy

STOP !

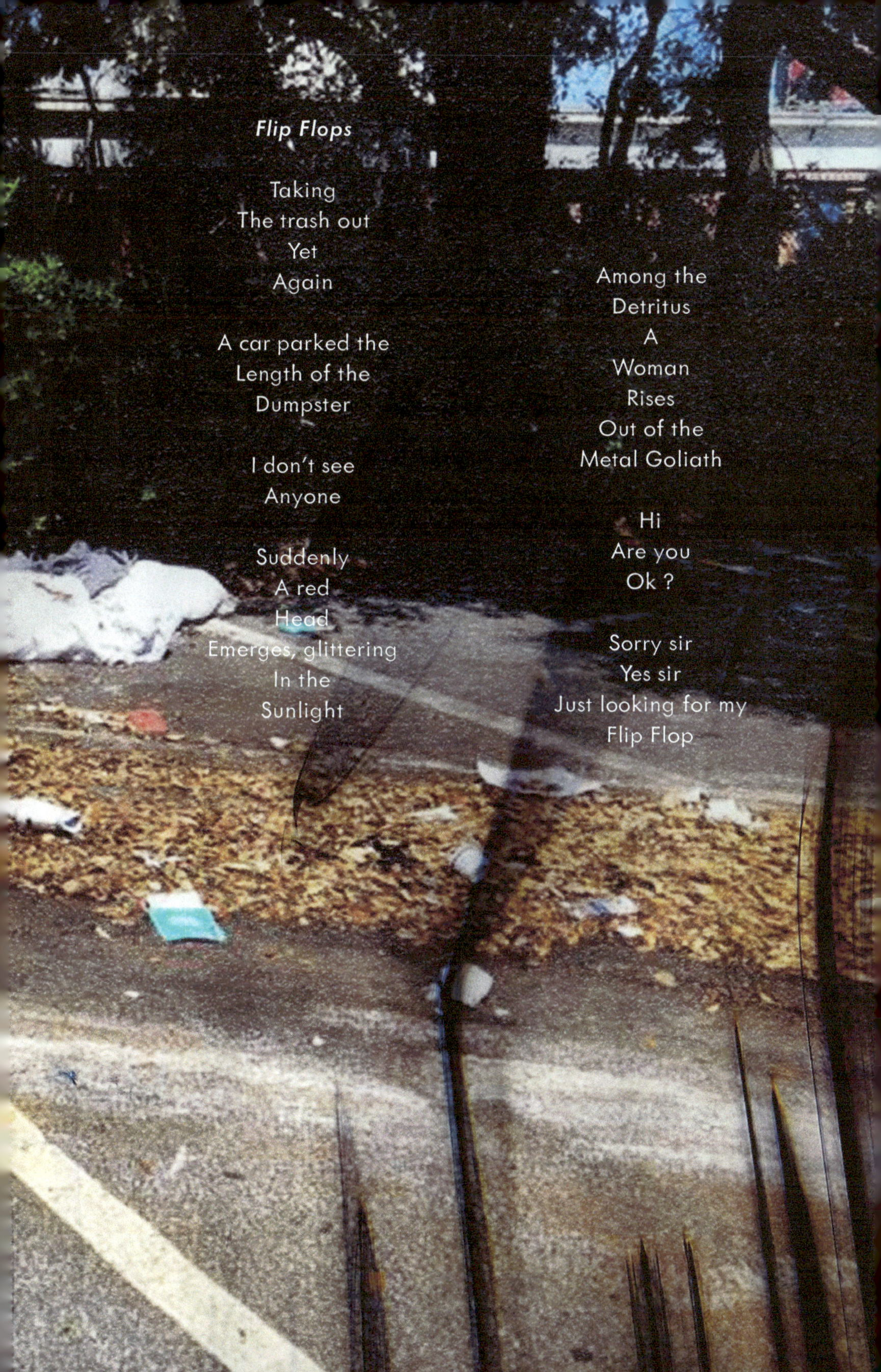

Flip Flops

Taking
The trash out
Yet
Again

A car parked the
Length of the
Dumpster

I don't see
Anyone

Suddenly
A red
Head
Emerges, glittering
In the
Sunlight

Among the
Detritus
A
Woman
Rises
Out of the
Metal Goliath

Hi
Are you
Ok ?

Sorry sir
Yes sir
Just looking for my
Flip Flop

The Whole Face

Employees

If you choose to
Wear a
Mask
At this time

And it is only covering
Your mouth

You are not
Wearing
It

Correctly

Frontline Heroes

Discount Day April 2

Special thanks to all first responders

He Has Risen

Fuck you
Cadbury egg
Man

50% off
And you
Are
Arguing over
20
Cents

Get out
You
Petty
Bastard

6ft.

Crack Head
Lamentations

6ft of
Distance

I haven't
Measured between
The
Registers
But it is
Inches

We now have
Partitions

For your safety

So you will
Be

Ok

473

How many
Times

Am I going
To take trash
To the
Dumpster

And throw it
On
A
Person

Who is completely
Inside this
Festering and rusted
Behemoth

Looking for
Receipts
So they can
Return
Shit
They never bought
In the first
Place

Single Use Only

Checking out

Next to me

I Just NEED the sale

Paper mask
BLACK
Around the
Nose
And
Mouth

Single
Use
Only

Products Of Fear

Do you have
Any

Hand Sanitizer ?

NO

Florida Blues

Customer:

I quit
Wearing
My
Mask

It's HOT in
The
Car

I can't
See
Where I'm
Going

It's

Dangerous

Inflation Is A Bitch

*How much are
The masks ?*

The 50 count
Is
29.99

The 20 count
Is
12.99

FUCK YOU

You
Price gouging
Fucks !

A Picture Worth Everything

I saw a
Corpse
Today

No less
Disturbing

Because it
Was a

Glossy photograph

Gary Humphrey,

This one is for you. I know you are rocking out with
the aliens and watching hockey with Bigfoot.

I love you,
Always

(photo by Anna Hubbard)

About the Author

Benjamin Embry loves all things horror. He has a masters degree in literature and creative writing and lives in Pensacola, Florida with his wife and two cat children.